Zoetry

A collection of poetic verse

Lillian Jade

Zoetry a collection of poetic verse

copyright © 2012 by Lillian Jade

ISBN-13: 978-0984879717
ISBN-10: 0984879714

Illustrated by Lillian Jade
Interior design by Laurie LaMonica-Szostak

Published by ZenLife Press
A Division of ZenLife, Inc.
New York
Printed in U.S.A.

To contact author:
lillianjade1019@gmail.com
Author's blog: www.lillianjade.com

Acknowledgments

I offer my grace to all of those whom so diligently believed in and supported the work of this collection.

As life is left to interpretation, poetry, for me, paints a tapestry of words yet unspoken. Words in colors of green and lavender paint my grace.

Lillian Jade

Table of Contents

Love

Running

Forgotten

Lost in mornings dew
a silent moment of truth
my forgotten rose
I weep for you...

Lillian Jade

Breath

All things have repose
as one door opens
life unfolds
fingers paint across my breath...

Abandon

Abandoning this life,
standing for a time with my bones,
un-fleshed force roamed free,
in the wind,
I watched, as you watched me

Nothing left, but breath now leaving,
as the eye looks everywhere to find,
a place, to once again,
begin believing...

The Dance

If I told you the pain is just part of the healing,
    would you dare to dance with me?
if I turned up life's melody,
letting all the world know, broken hearts can be remade

Would you dance in the wake of the storm,
as waves crash against the shore
where my brokenness has brought me?
The coolness of air, a source of my healing,
arms reaching, nature teaching,
trees become my strength in weakness,
the refuge that I seek

Would you dare to come blindly, and dance with me
on a teardrop composed of memory,
of a place I've never known,
of a song of how it's suppose to be?

Would you dare to climb onto the teardrop, and dance
    with me,
on a leaf atop a tree,
floating into the air carelessly?

Zoetry

Would you barefoot dare to dance with me
in the naked reality of all you see,
under the moon, footprints in the sand,
would you hold me close, as I touched your hand?

Would you dare to chance into my soul, and dance with me,
Un-inhibited and naked,
on an island just with me,
would you dare to be, the composer of the music needed,
    to dance with me?
Under a sunset of tranquility
all the world to see,
would you gently remove my glass slipper, and dance
    with me?
Removal of glass,
would it then set me free?

Escapade of Chance

A chance escapade
*   the birds serenade*
*   forgotten and befallen*
*   pauper and maid*

for the very first time
*   poetry sublime*
*   drunk on a kiss*
*   a cheap bottle of wine*

Life, just a little off key
*   you being you, me being me*
*   dancing by moonlight*
*   we drift out to sea*
*   you being you,*
*   me being me…*

Along the Shore

Revisiting pain,
a wave crashes,
a release of rain.
Cloud forms above,
sky
parts,
washing away,
tattoos on my heart...
Grace falls like rain...

Diamond

Shadows of doubt,
now kept at bay,
tweeting of birds,
the song that they play.
For all that comes,
with every cry,
all that washes,
with the tide.
The silenced words,
my breath you saw,
tasting my lips,
uncovered and raw.
Would you seek my pleasure
or remain in awe?
Would you lay with me
on a bed of rose,
if I asked of you,
would you shut life's door?
Dance naked amid,
imperfection and flaw?
Beg for forgiveness,
want nothing more?

Stand out in the rain,
under a summer's heat?
Life as a diamond...
perfectly complete

You Are

Scrape away the rust,
faded memories,
photographs,
now collect dust,
feeling the percussion,
of heart and breath,
just because I must.
Kiss me hard,
as my roots are deep,
no apologies,
no thank you card,
no words, no less,
wisdom of silence,
bask in the bliss,
of nothingness.
Opening of chest,
offering of breath,
no novice at life,
too often a guest,
falling to the ground,
not breaking sweat,
silent sound;
word, poem, kiss, pain

all collide in the rain.
For the hardest mile I have ever walked,
you are the poem I write,
the grace I wake,
the kiss I feel,
the reason I talk...

What Is Love

You who breathed along with me,
taking away the heartache.
Wanting to live like this,
warm breath on my face.
Hold the fight,
don't ask why.
In my thoughts,
I fly to you.
When I wake from the dream,
I weep for you.
Silvery moon over the sea,
waves are calm,
winds of my sail,
now set free.
In the night, holding me,
as all the world sleeps,
gazing at you,
amid fragranced air,
touched by your hand,
your feathered breath,
what is life.
If not the reason for love?

Tulip

Tulip reaching, takes a bow
held hand up,
if ever needing you,
it is now
Grace melts away the rain,
dew drops etched on breath,
heart harbors clouds,
shadows feel my strain
Air of anger,
sea of calm,
moment of surrender,
I flounder in the mercy of the sky
if you truly see my heart,
then I have exposed too much,
for you were never suppose to see, the I

You

My only love,
it is you, I hold in hand,
fingers delicate,
in a pure white glove.
Barren thorn of the rose,
you begin to bud.
Mirrored perfectly,
you are my poetry,
my desire,
you consume me,
like a wild fire,
on an African plain,
under an Amazon rain,
you are my witness,
in silence…
when words are not enough…

Your Perfume

When angels dance
on moonlight nights,
storm clouds clear,
shaping all thats right.
Shaded,
jaded,
muted,
subdued,
the sting of life,
the perfume of you.

Tiles

Mosaic tiles
paint my life,
a stain glass view
    who more naked than I
    on the breaking sun,
    on a mornings dew?
        Trees whisper
        a contented green,
        moments of clouds,
        a photograph,
        unforeseen dream
            Happily haunted
            by loving ghosts,
            some days alone
            facing the sea,
            waves silently moan
                Suddenly so young
                the lyric inside me,
                yet to be sung
                    Photographs die
                    revealing a print,
                    mirrored face
                    fertile rain,
                    wash the tear
                    of unknown place

Filling my ears
a birds instrument,
as words fall still
and poems fade,
dawn to dusk now spent
> *Bodies entwine*
> *passions delight,*
> *dew of your breath,*
> *we eclipse the night*
>> *Softness of flesh*
>> *forever embraced,*
>> *romantic slumbering,*
>> *a kiss well placed*
>>> *Pearls of your body*
>>> *seducing and caught,*
>>> *stolen glimpses,*
>>> *of forbidden thought*
>>>> *In the vast of stillness*
>>>> *we awake the kiss,*
>>>> *as our breaths collide*
>>>> *in mystical mist*

Fire

Heart is heaviest when in reprieve,
tears forgotten
wiped on sleeve,
softer than summer air,
night time dreams
daylight slumber,
morning's mist on sullen tree,
clouds lay thick,
on memory.
Stay for awhile, as night depart
harp and arrow,
hand in heart,
night time kisses, left in air,
stroke of cheek
brush of hair.
Love have no fear, have no tire,
place of hand,
fulfill desire,
as sin is mirrored,
we light the fire.

I Am

I am half
I am whole
I am young
I am old
I am weak
I am strong
I am mirrored
I am bold.
I am sang
I am sung
Without breath
Without lung
I am poem
I am verse
I am rhythm
I am curse
I am all that you want me to be.

Ballerina Pose

Your sheet music
sprawled across the sky,
stars kiss my cheek tonight,
in slumber, I close my eyes

Blessed by your breath,
loosing thought to air,
sleeping like a ballerina,
floating without care,
freezing mid kiss on your melting stare,
as you drift away, in my rivers deep,
floating through my bloodstream,
a love letter, I now keep

Dare

Dance with me,
on a river of rock,
by the edge of the sea,
in absence of fear,
barefoot on a beach,
in open delight,
under the stars,
in the dark of the night.

Dance with me,
on the stillness of air,
on the wave of my breath,
naked and raw,
as my bodies flesh,
is all you saw.

Dance with me,
do you dare,
or is my naked reality
too much to bare?

Lillian Jade

The Rose

Felt your breath
caress my hair,
in that moment
of captured stare,
my heart was open
your hands were free,
I asked for nothing
you gave me, me.
Shared my secrets
harbored my pain,
planted a rose
out in the rain,
the wind blew,
storm poured down,
we saved each other,
but the rose drowned.
Picked up the seedlings
to begin anew,
found fertile soil
and then it grew,
water and ice,
snow and rain,
fire and heat
we overcame.

Seasons changed
as time went by,
I lie with the rose
and question why?

Fantasy Lover

Leaves sat still,
in you flew,
breaking not sound,
on my window sill

Left one of your feathers,
next to your note,
you flew away,
leaving only,
your red-breasted overcoat

Can You?

Can you feel the poetry of a summers rain?
Can you feel the poetry of a lover's pain?
Can you feel the poetry of life's embrace?
Can you feel my passion of leather and lace?

> Can you move inside me, on a rising tide?
> Can you move my breath, a river wide?
> Can you move the thought, arise my soul?
> Can you free the ME, that someone stole?

The Giving

You,
brought forth
to me
a new surrendering

Dreams,
I never dreamed
words,
I never spoke
Breath
I never breathed
thought,
never provoked

Portrait,
I never painted
color,
I never saw
Songs,
I never sang
sensuality,
never so open and raw

Zoetry

You,
gave
to me
renderings

Rhythm,
I never danced
book,
I never read
touch,
I never felt
kiss,
never such, have I ever bled

You
gave
to me

Lover

In another life,
perhaps we'll meet,
unborn leaves,
beneath our feet,
we'll tip toe through,
a summers heat,
lips embraced,
in a final greet

Body Heat

Curve of my body
pressed against yours

Tips of my breasts
touching your heart

Hipbones lifted
space now filled

Arousal of plenty
sensation now
stilled

Forgotten

Sometimes,
it hurts,
more than I want it to.
Reflection,
is
mirrored glass.
Tear
that floats,
is yours to frame.
Picture
perfect portrait,
of tireless game.
Tear left,
of ill regrets,
forgotten pain.
I remember,
I remember your name.
It was you,
who forgot the same.
Your imprint
left,
on my bed,
your ghostly stain.

Glass of Wine

Ruby red,
velvet,
crossing over lips.

Traveling,
the passage,
to a dance.

In my throat,
sweet and wet,
mellow and dry.

Glass of wine,
the blood of my circulatory,
I quench on your delight.

Pouring a glass,
dribbles of,
compulsive confidence,
I write.

Dream

It was blue
It was pink
It was greenest green
It was yellow
It was lavender
It was reddest red
It was orange
It was purple
It was white
It was turquoise
It was marooned maroon
It was pure
It was simple
Exotic and sweet
It was lure
It was lust
It was pageantry of fuss
It was fantasy
It was fiction
It was my dream of must
    The colors arrived,
    the vision was clear
    Dreams took flight,
    from dawn to dusk

My dream became,
the color of a rainbow
The edge of a cusp

Child of Mine

As day grew long,
and night grew cold,
I sang you a lullaby,
of fairy tale told,
watching your breath,
caressing your fears,
wiping away rain,
through tear stained years.
Child of mine,
innocent, naive,
take hold of my hand,
as your life you weave,
when you are lost,
amid a distant land,
paint your life,
paintbrush in hand.
Symphony of color,
is yours to choose,
not black and white,
but a pattern of hues.
Child of mine,
tell me your dreams,
the future you seek,
escapades and schemes.

Child of mine,
brave and now bold,
remember the time,
of fairy tale told.
Now put on your shoes,
open life's door,
know I will love you,
forever, forever more

Lullaby

A child,
as angels speak,
falls to slumber,
falls to sleep.
Shaded colors,
rainbow schemes,
innocent, naive,
fairyland dreams.
Tomorrow awaits,
sleep the night,
hush lullaby,
'till mornings light.
Sprinkling moonbeams,
from up high,
scaring away monsters,
wiping your eyes.
Melody,
of moon beam sky,
twinkle, twinkle,
fairy dust and lullabies,
fall asleep hush don't cry…

Child

Every child,
a poem born out of
heavenly sound,
towering cathedrals,
as we, mere mortals,
gather on the ground

Motherhood

Words fell silent,
from your tongue,
as we got old,
your bitter became young

Emptiness, of wombs embrace,
stoic stern, seen on your face,
motherhood, a torture,
You, a stranger in that place

Only now,
I come to see,
motherhood, was not for you,
what it was for me
You, you saw it
as your curse
I, I wore it
as my vintage purse

Son

She stole your heart,
in perfect haiku

Church bells chimed,
the man you grew

You gave the ring,
said I do

Gathering no moss,
then you flew

For me,
a moment
of saddened blue

Red Robin

Come run with me
tell me of life,
of distant dreams and mirrored faces
shattered glass
masquerade places

Of unchartered course
distant shores,
of timid day
a lion's roar

Come Red Robin
perch on my knee,
untie my laces
run with me

The keeper of my secrets,
so you be...

Untold Whisper

Embracing a journey,
sweat on my brow,
dance in my feet,
I'm partial
I'm whole,
not nearly complete.
Changing life,
as it changes me,
winter to spring,
endless summer's heat.
Rhythm of feet,
breath of my soul,
heart carries secrets,
yet untold,
life as a whisper,
yet to unfold…

Tree

Tree of life
you sway so green,
amid the air
on mornings glaze

Copper tones
now turn to gold,
yellow and red
foliage ablaze

Autumn eclipsing
from summers haze,
change in color
is your parade

Puddles Appearance

The puddle,
embraces
me,
tortures
me,
envelopes
me,
bequeaths
me,
surrounds
me,
sings
to me,
stars
at me,
holds
me,
soothes
me,
surprises me,
with dampness on my flesh

Rivers Stream

So vast,
wide,
long,
deep,
cascading
over rock,
crashing
along the shore,
riding
my tide,
pulsating
my soul,
momentum of the river brings me life

Snowflake

Snowflake
melting
in
my
hand.

I
tried to
hold
you, so
perfectly.

Alas,
you
have
faded
to memory.

I Think

I think, I spy the sea
dipped beyond the tree

I think, I see the moon
as it stares back at me

I think, I feel my breath
as sweat I let it be

I think, I feel my feet
as body lends to heat

I think, of roads less traveled
the lessons that they've lent

I think the world lays silent
neither I, nor sparrow, break the spent

Bareness

Out to sea
leaving the day on the shore
wild, relentless, free,
who could want for anything more
skinny dipping
in the bareness of me

Bluebird

Would your lullaby
    eclipse the night
        as you the bluebird
            flies into my sight?

Would arms wrap around
    lifting my core
        wiping the tear
            of the pain that I bore?

Would you hum the song
    in absence of words
        lay by me side
            with my blood on your sword?

Open your wings
    in expansion of flight
        as dusk turns to dawn
            and darkness to light.

Would you bluebird
    open my eyes
        revel with sight
            turning all thats wrong
                into all thats right?

Bluebird, bluebird
        lend me a wing
                on an unopened prayer
                        as all the world sleeps
                                and I in your care.

Would you menace me none
        and forget me not
                or fly away, fly away
                        and deepen the plot?

Lillian Jade

Seasons Change (So Do We)

Cyclical air,
breath surrounds,
leaves perish,
upon the ground
Summers heat,
loosing touch,
falls parade,
stampede of must
Winters cold
soon to follow,
flakes surprise,
in purest sorrow
Spring awakes,
silent sound,
tulips tongue,
in rebound
Cycles of life
in constant view,
change in a moment,
on sudden queue
Beneath the tree,
the leaf,

the tulip,
winters flake,
in childlike hope, of fantasy

Lillian Jade

A Stroke

Wanting to die,
with folded arms,
I close my eyes,
drifting lifeless,
into forever,
purple violet,
red green,
colors of,
my final dream
Tear stained eye,
empty glances,
please don't cry,
I lie asleep,
in perfect die
No rhythm of heart,
no beat of soul,
wiping a final tear,
from the corner of eye,
breath releasing
a final sigh
To life, I solemnly wave goodbye

Death Do Us Part

Things fall silent,
eternal rest,
thoughts now linger,
no one longer,
weeps for us.
Photographs die,
blueprint of face,
rain now falling,
this forgotten place.

Self

Self, under a cloud filled sky,
the mind a voyage,
birds await a butterfly.
> An unloved person doesn't die,
> he withers like an unused hand,
> as we sit in silence, and question the why.
> > We hide safely, in our own needs,
> > bartering gifts for life,
> > as the sea of tide recedes.

Ever Changing

Willows whisper,
in the wind,
pages turn,
lovers stray,
all things pass,
then move away.

Cancer

Raging,
deep inside,
no time to turn,
no time to hide

A price paid,
for a life
of choosing,
angels speak,
on
twilights cruising

Breath is hushed,
not a sound,
clouds suspend,
no longer ground

Peace in death,
as there you lay,
arms cross over,
in final pray

Zoetry

An angelic whisper,
words fall silent,
body still,
all is dark,
it is now Gods will

Sword of light,
now leads your way,
gone from here,
gone from stay

Loosing touch,
feel of hand,
imprint left,
along the sand

Bequeath your thought

Pain

Grief,
breaks upon my feet,
as pebbles of pain,
I release,
and pass from suffering,
holding face,
within my palm,
my weeps of sorrow,
now muffling,
as crackles of sound
drown from me,
and barter down,
I sit and pray.

Heaven

I know a place,
where angels fly,
where tattered hearts,
are kissed goodbye.
I know a place,
that leaps the sky,
where fear is left,
and said goodbye.
Heaven waits,
for you and I.

Lillian Jade

When I am Gone

And so,
when time has stopped,
in eternal sound,
what will they say,
what words be found,
as I am placed,
in final ground?

Will they lay a kiss,
upon my face,
fold my hands,
in final place,
in eternity,
hold my grace?
or lie a veil of feathered lace,
across their tears,
to hide disgrace?

Memory

Fragile and innocent,
quiet and safe,
in instant surrender,
to time and place,
feel my breath,
hold my hand,
times hour glass,
is loosing sand.
Silent rain,
wash over me,
northern star,
forever free.
Clouds brought rain,
at you I stare,
holding my rose,
amid perfumed air.
Dreams unraveled,
silence spoke,
how many deaths did we die,
before we awoke?

Where

Where do nightmares go
when night turns to dawn?
Where do daydreams go
when day turns to dusk?
What happens to a life
when all is broken down?
What happens to me
when I am to lost to be found?

Set Free

Pure abandon,
tide washes,
carries me,
out to sea,
crumpled photograph,
faded memory,
faded me,
a salted breath,
now sets me free

All Things

Of all things lost,
all is found,
unsung song,
touch without sound,
breaking night,
with thunderous ground.
Sleep in peace,
for tomorrow comes.

Lies

From one end to the other,
nothing to hide,
as sea takes shape,
I begin to glide

A moment or two,
amid cloudless sky,
as self disappears,
patterned palette of lies

Breath in a capsule,
of borrowed time,
rhythm of feet,
all the world is mine,
riding the sea,
on a mirage of tide

What Is To Be?

The sky reflects the sea
master of what is to be,
the bird, my puppet, serenading me
looking at tomorrow,
mist lies in yesterday,
the words I did not say,
the gentle touch you could not find
nameless faces
forever blind.
Some dreams are destined to remain,
a private sanctuary, never claimed,
can't stay forever in the rain,
light plays off a puddle,
personal portrait of pain.
Quiet isolation,
sheltered coves,
consistent winds,
life explored,
in this moment,
jaded and unsure,
thoughts needing an open door.

Sky parts,
through the rain I see,
finally I recognize,
the reflection is me…

Letting Go

Past imperfections,
sorrow and pain,
forgotten kisses,
left in the rain

Past mistakes,
and early sins,
all things lost,
and lonely wins

Life gone wrong,
all that's right,
careless days,
sleepless nights

Endless worries,
frozen fear,
stolen glances,
jealous sneer,

Took awhile
to understand,
can't recall when or why,
letting go, lets you fly

Mermaid

Running free,
rain washes memory,
accepting all that is to be,
life no longer a shrouded mystery,
opening eyes fully to see,
mermaid standing in front of me,
swimming free,
all her fears now out to sea,
as sand and salt anchor me,
an appealing view of purity

You Are Gone

Heard the train,
pull into the station,
couldn't wait,
to see,
your face

Saw the doors close,
sound of the engine,
as it pulled away,
I stood,
waiting

I waited,
for your face,
and how your hair,
always,
fell in a cascade of waves

I waited,
for your silhouette,
to appear,
the edge,
of chiseled jaw

I waited,
for your voice,
to sound,
vibrations,
from your lips

I waited,
to run to you,
the embrace,
jumping,
into your arms

I waited,
as a train pulled,
into the station,
screeching,
to a halt

I waited,
doors flew open,
searched for you,
pressed my face,
looking through the glass

I waited,
I am still waiting,
for you

Flesh

Sand
penetrates my toes

Waves crash
along the shore

Mind wanders
to place unknown

Ships pass
leaving someone alone

Sitting
in the sand,
all I am,
is flesh and bones

My breath leaves on a wave

Casting

Atonement comes in quiet places
untouched words
forgotten faces
no farewell left behind
as breath and sneakers
together glide
allowing answers
to grow inside
casting fear into the tide
My morning's perfect run

Lillian Jade

Distant Shores

Distant lands,
brand new places,
untold tales,
unknown faces

Dove in hand,
bird in tree,
on this land,
running free

The land is vast,
river wide,
out stretched arms,
open stride

Rounding bend,
where once began,
forever grounded,
where I stand

Reminding me,
of time and space,
clouds dissipate,
before my face

Wind is calm,
strength is strong,
day is quiet,
as road is long

Etched in sky,
breath becomes,
purest paint,
eternal Swan song

Driftwood

Seeing the ocean
starring into the sky,
pondering life's questions,
just my sneakers and I

The calm of the sea
against soft winded breath,
sand penetrates my toes,
salt spray rests on flesh

Imprints lay restless
on yesterdays sand,
a sea maidens journey,
as I step off land

I part with my sneakers
swim into the sea,
the world now lays quiet,
driftwood bare and barren, now carries me

Thoughts

Thought I cared about the moon,
the stars,
thought I lived within my dreams,
thought the stillness of the night,
brought the surrendering,
turns out it brought the dawn
letting go of my blanket,
for the crisp of morning air,
feet now delivered to the pavement,
as flesh opens on the sun

My Morning Run

If my sneakers could talk,
they'd tell you a tale,
of innocence lost,
broken and frail,
of morning dew,
and scarlet night,
of sweat on brow,
and heart of fright,
of dreams elapsed,
a rose petal tear,
secrets with birds,
entrancement of deer,

Of all that is found,
when all is lost,
deafening silence,
paying the cost,

Of cascading moonbeams,
golden red sunsets,
a wish on a star,
a promise now kept,
of nakedly running,
in a Caribbean sea,
of tracing footsteps,
in the sand of me,
if only my sneakers could talk

My Tapestry

I am the deer today,
I am the red cardinal perched on tree,
I am the sway of tree,
I am the dew on grass,
I am the reflection on river,
I am the path beneath my feet.
I am the rainbow,
I am shattered glass,
I am the tapestry I paint.
I am the tear running down as nature's cry,
I am the unfolding spring, and the tormented winter,
I am the puddles and the ice.
The snowflake that once melted on my tongue,
I am the wisdom of birds in flight,
I am everything and all, as I run carelessly.
I am floating,
I am flying,
my legs have taken on life.
I am inside out,
I am outside in,
I am leather and lace,
I am passion and sin,
the careless forbidden, bite of the sting.

The Burn

Running hard,
sweating wildly,
my skin burns underneath,
to a soft pear, cooked to a boil
Bird flys up,
breathing the sugar smell of my skin,
now thirsting for my salt

Sculpture

Architectural veil
of my existence

Columns
of my body

Poetry
of my mind

Wetness
of my breath

Coveting
of my bareness

Harnessing
of my heart

Molding
of my sculpture

The clay is still wet

Lillian Jade

Dried Petals

A single,
long stemmed rose,
soft velvet

Coated,
in morning's dew

A thoughtful linger,
remembrance of you

Tip of my finger,
pierced by thorn

Broken Heart,
life now torn

Turned the page,
closed the book

Crumpled dry,
years it took

A dried rose,
now lays

Zoetry

Years have past,
since those days

I've since,
turned life's page

Morning

Never as I was before,
each time I step
outside my door.
Never you thought
you knew me,
never you thought
me you saw.
I am no more,
from dark of night,
I run on open shore,
never the I in me
no more.

Hush, I silently
close the door,
tracing bones
across my face,
blood pools in cheek,
breath rides a wave,
sweat arrives
in aromatic lure.

Zoetry

Mornings air,
I've waited for,
feet hit ground
in submissive secure,
I escape,
through an open door.
You'll find me
at the river,
thirsting on my pour,
curvature of breath,
peeking through,
in abandoned raw.
Never as I was,
never no more,
Rapture of running through,
morning's open door.

Prose

If I only knew,
who would have thought?

Forgiveness of breath,
embrace now caught

Flower petal,
scent of a rose

Ligament of leg,
a silent pose

Who would have thought,
the awake of the prose?

Would be inside me,
waiting on reveal

Who could have known,
to open its seal